WELCOME TO THE ARNOL BLACKF

Arnol – the name may derive from *hraun-holl*, 'stony hill or ridge' – has a settlement history reaching back more than 2000 years. And yet the houses forming the present township, *baile*, have only been in their current positions for a little over a century. They include the two blackhouses, *taighean-dubha*, at nos. 39 and 42 Arnol.

Change is an inevitable part of life, to be accepted not deplored, but it is important to understand and appreciate the main stages of cultural development. The kind of culture represented by these two blackhouses was a very long and basic stage in the history of Highland and Island Scotland, and both will now remain an enduring symbol and reflection of a form of community organisation that in another generation will lie quite outside the memory of individuals.

Above
The blackhouse at no. 42 Arnol and (behind) the white house that replaced it as the MacLeod family's residence in 1966.

CONTENTS

Left: David and Christine MacLeod, the builders of no. 42 Arnol, pose for the camera in front of their peat stack.

ARNOL AT A GLANCE

For hundreds of years, it was the custom in Lewis for man and beast to be housed under the same roof. When no. 42 Arnol was vacated in the 1960s, the thatched blackhouse was entrusted into state care. Today, it is the last tangible link with that tradition, and visiting it evokes a form of living and working on Lewis that now lies outwith the memory of individuals.

Two aspects of a blackhouse make it very different from a modern house – it was a residence for animals as well as people, and there was no chimney. Having animals 'living in' had its advantages. It made the house warmer and meant fewer buildings were needed. The smoke rising from the peat fire into the roof also had hidden benefits. It killed bugs, and the smoke-laden thatch made excellent fertiliser for the fields.

Right: The blackhouse and croft at no. 42 in July 1966.

A TIME CAPSULE

12 AT THE FIRE
The peat fire was the centre of family life and never allowed to go out. Here the family cooked, ate, sat, relaxed and entertained.

14 A GOOD NIGHT'S SLEEP
The family slept in three cosy box-beds.

17 IN THE BYRE
The family's cows 'lived in' with them over the winter.

27 IN THE 'WHITE HOUSE'
The family at no. 39 moved into their new 'white house' in the 1920s.

A SUSTAINABLE BUILDING

14 WOOD
With wood in scarce supply, crofters recycled parts from old boats as roof timbers.

21 STONE
They built the blackhouse walls from stone cleared from the land and used peat-mould as cavity-wall insulation.

23 STRAW
They thatched the roof with oatstraw surplus from the harvest.

23 HEATHER
They covered the thatch in a 'hair net' of heather rope, weighted down with stones, to stop the wind blowing it away.

A HARD DAY'S WORK

HARVEST HOME

3

A PERSONAL IMPRESSION

Blackhouses seem more archaic than they really are. Their architecture and layout carry on traditions of a form of living and working that is infinitely older. This was what impressed itself most strongly during my first visit to no. 42 Arnol in May 1964, when the house was still occupied.

The single door in the long front wall led into an area where some brown hens were kept. Immediately opposite, a second door opened into the barn. On the right there was a door through to the byre, where a young beast lay in a stall, bedded on straw. To the left, the door opening to the living room was partly covered by a wire-netting frame to keep out the hens. In the centre of the stone and clay floor, a fire of peat smouldered with a steady, red glow from which rose not so much smoke as a smoky shimmer of heat, with no chimney to draw it out. The reek of burning peat filled the air with warmth, adding an evocative dimension to the atmosphere.

Here three generations lived together, who spoke only Gaelic among themselves, in a blackhouse that provided ample warmth and shelter. By day the living room was the centre for the everyday domestic jobs of the women – mending clothes, preparing food for themselves, the hens and the calves, washing dishes. But the evening was the great time, when the whole family reassembled, and people dropped in, to sit in social relaxation round the fire, the focal point of the whole house. Relaxed, but not necessarily idle, for spinning, wool-winding and knitting kept the women busy and the men might wind ropes out of freshly pulled heather fronds, or mend a broken creel.

There is here a sense of pleasure in social communion, a sense that came through clearly also on my day-time visit. Mingling with this, on my first sight of the blackhouse living room, was an awareness that this was a glimpse of a culture nearing its end, becoming part of Scotland's historical past.

Professor Alexander Fenton

Director, European Ethnological Research Centre

Above: Photographs of no. 42 Arnol taken in 1966 shortly after the MacLeod family moved to their new white house next door.

1 Outside the blackhouse.

2 The living room looking towards the bedroom.

3 The byre.

Right: Kirsty Campbell (seated) and Mr. MacCalum at the fire in Mrs. Campbell's blackhouse elsewhere in Arnol in 1937.

'Very often after tea an old woman comes in for a ceilidh you know just to gossip. I remember a few years ago when my uncle was at home from Canada, people used to come every night. What time we had, singing and many other sources of entertainment.'

'Glè thrice' thigeadh cailleach a-steach a chèilidh dìreach airson faighinn a-mach dè a bha a' dol. Tha cuimhne agam o chionn bliadhna no dhà air ais an uair a bha bràthair m' athar aig an taigh à Canada, b'àbhaist daoine a bhith a' tighinn a chèilidh a h-uile oidhche. Abair toileachas, a' seinn agus ri iomadh cur-seachad eile.'

From a young girl's reminiscences recorded in *West Side Story*, 1964

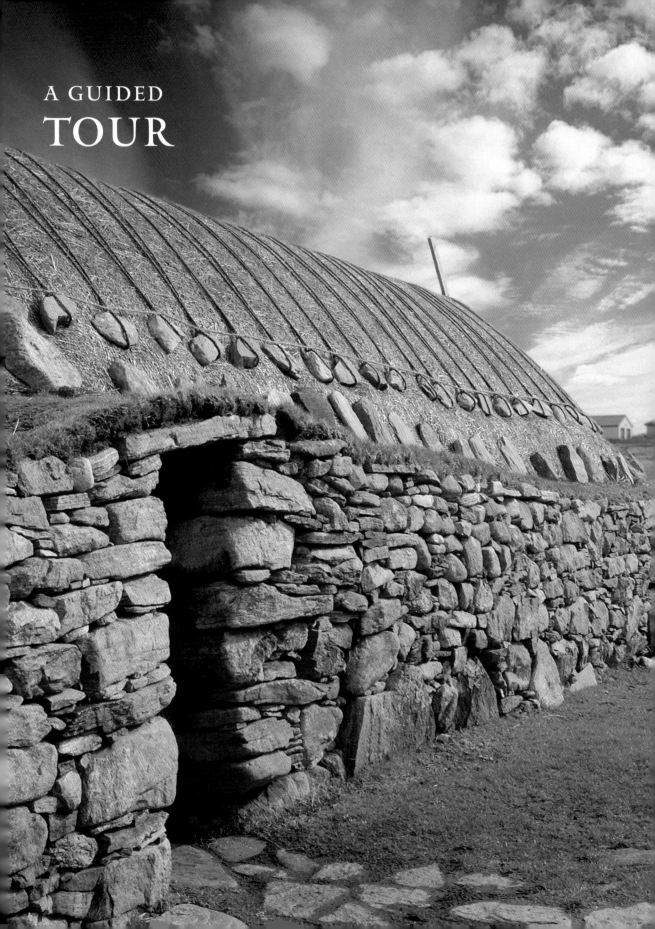

A GUIDED
TOUR

A GUIDED TOUR

This guided tour takes you around the complex of blackhouses and white houses belonging to no. 39 and no. 42 Arnol.

The tour begins at the BLACKHOUSE OF NO. 42. (1) This was built around 1880 and lived in until 1966. During those 80 years, the property underwent only slight modification, and you will see it much as it was left when the family moved out.

The tour then takes you across the road to the CROFT AT NO. 39. The unroofed blackhouse here (2), built a little before 1880, displays subtle differences to no. 42. It was also vacated somewhat earlier, around 1930, when the family moved into the new WHITE HOUSE (3) beside it. The latter, internally and externally, still looks today much as it did when the last resident moved out in 1976.

Your tour ends back in the VISITOR CENTRE (4). This building too is part of the story, for it was originally the white house at no. 42, into which the family from the adjacent blackhouse moved in 1966. It ceased to be a residence in 1997.

Visitors are advised to mind their heads when moving about both blackhouses, as the ceilings are low. Also take care when crossing the road between the two crofts - it is a public road!

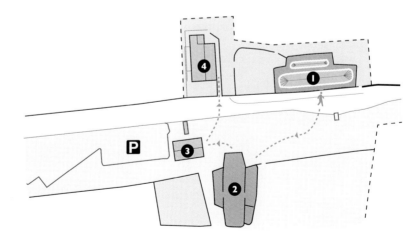

Left
The visitor centre (4) built in 1966 to replace the blackhouse at no. 42 Arnol as the family residence.

Above
Site plan showing the route of the guided tour.

Opposite page
The front door into the blackhouse (1) at no. 42 Arnol.

Key to numbers
1 No. 42 Arnol - blackhouse
2 No. 39 Arnol - blackhouse
3 No. 39 Arnol - white house
4 No. 42 Arnol - white house (now visitor centre)

THE BLACKHOUSE AT NO. 42 ARNOL

The blackhouse at no. 42 Arnol is a unique and precious relic the residence of a Hebridean crofting family, and their animals, preserved almost as the family left it when they moved out in 1966. When the state took guardianship of the blackhouse shortly after, there was a good number of Hebridean blackhouses still in use as homes; today there is none. When the last blackhouse was vacated, a way of life reaching far back into the past came to an end. That is why no. 42 Arnol is unique and precious; it is much more than just a thatched house – it remains the sole representative of a way of life once so common but now altogether gone.

No. 42 Arnol was a family home for around 80 years, and during that time the family made modest changes. Some were DIY home improvements (for example, the bedroom window); others were forced upon them (such as the shortening of the barn, apparently after a sea–mine exploded around 1940). Since coming into state care, necessary repairs have been made, principally to the roof, but essentially what the visitor sees today is what existed in 1966.

Right: The living room in the blackhouse looking towards the byre.

Below left: The living room in 1966. The walls and part of the roof were formerly covered with wallpaper.

Below right: The dresser and plate-rack in the living room. The top of the plate-rack is angled to match the slope of the roof.

'the peat fire was the centre of family life
and was never allowed to go out'

'B,'e an teine-monach cridhe beatha an teaghlaich agus cha
bhithe a' leigeil leis a dhol às uair sam bith.'

THE THRESHOLD *An stairsneach*

The front door, *dorus*, leads into an entrance area, *dol-a-steach* (literally 'going in'). Both people and cattle had to use this entrance, but whereas in older blackhouses the front door opened straight into the byre, late nineteenth-century blackhouses such as no. 42 have an enclosed threshold separating living room from byre. In 1964, this area was used as the henhouse.

The present roof, *mullach tighe*, has been restored. The rafters, *na ceanglaichean*, linked by single tie-beams, *sparran*, cross at the apex to make a cradle for the roof-ridge, *gath droma*. The tie-beams are fixed by wooden pins to the rafters. Each horizontal purlin, *taobhan*, is made of separate lengths of wood lashed together, such was the scarcity of timber on Lewis. In fact, above the door you will see a large oar re-used as a rafter.

...🚶 Enter through the front door facing onto the road.

Right: The threshold viewed from the door into the barn.

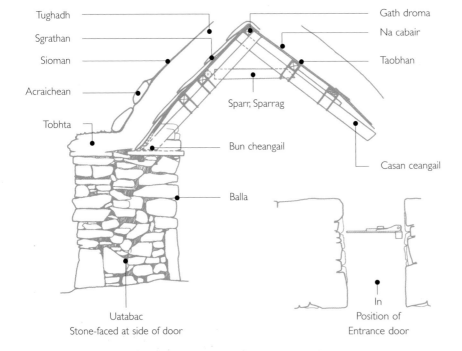

Tughadh

Sgrathan

Sioman

Acraichean

Tobhta

Gath droma

Na cabair

Taobhan

Sparr, Sparrag

Bun cheangail

Casan ceangail

Balla

In

Uatabac
Stone-faced at side of door

Position of
Entrance door

Left: Cross section through the entrance showing the building construction.

Gaelic terms:
uatabac *(tempered earth-core)*
balla *(wall)*
tobhta *(wall ledge)*
casan ceangail *(roof couple)*
bun cheangail *(couple foot)*
acraichean *(anchor stones)*
sparr, sparrag *(tie beam)*
sioman *(rope)*
sgrath, sgrathan *(turf, turves)*
tughadh *(thatch)*
taobhan *(purlin)*
na ceanglaichean *(roof timbers)*
gath droma *(roof ridge)*

THE LIVING ROOM *Aig an teine*

To the left of the threshold is the living room, *aig an teine* (literally 'at the fire'). It is entered through a wooden partition which has a half-door. The opening was once screened by a wire-netting frame to keep the hens out.

In the centre of the living-room floor is the central hearth, *cagailt*. A drain, *eisir*, appears to run right underneath it, for in wet weather dampness from the drain can be seen rising from the sand in which the hearth stones are bedded.

The iron links, *slabhraidh*, and crook, *dubhan*, from which the pots and kettle were hung, are fastened to the roof-ridge, the strongest part of the roof-timbers. The rest of the floor is roughly paved with flagstones. The walls were formerly covered with wallpaper, extending up the walls and a third of the way up the soot-blackened rafters of the roof.

Above: Upright butter churn. The family also had a rotary butter churn.

Top: The living room, with the settle beside the fire.

The living room contains the basic blackhouse furnishings. There is nothing lavish about them; functionalism rather than ornament was the prime consideration. They tended to be substantially but plainly made of wood, painted or varnished a dark colour – usually brown. All the furniture is ranged along the side walls, leaving as much space as possible around the central hearth.

Along the left-hand wall is the settle, *being*. Two drawers occupy half its length, whilst the other half, left open for storing articles such as footwear underneath, is curtained across at the front. At the end of the settle nearest the door is a low cupboard, *preas*, that held the food supplies. Formerly, there was a dresser, *dreasar*, for bed-covers and blankets at the other end.

Along the right-hand wall is a cupboard, a dresser with a well-shaped top and the unusual feature of two built-in mirrors, and another more traditional type of dresser and plate-rack. The dresser with mirrors is not local but was bought in Edinburgh shortly after World War I. The number of dressers in the house was unusual for a blackhouse. Other items include an iron girdle, *grideal*, for baking, a tinker's lamp, *lampa cheaird* (often used in the byre during milking), an upright churn, *biota*, and a hanger, *cloran*, made from the dried and hardened stem and leaf-stalks of a kind of thistle that grows in sandy soil.

In the far wall opposite the entrance is a box-bed, *leabaidh dhuinte*, one of three in the house. It is curtained off from the living room.

Above: The family kettle, forever on the boil.

Below

1 Tinker's lamp, used in the byre during milking.

2 Coat hangers made from thistle stems.

3 Ceramic jug.

4 Assorted jars and crockery.

THE BEDROOM *A' Chulaist*

A wooden partition, *tallan fiodha*, separates the living room from the bedroom, *a' Chulaist*. This is the only room with a wall window, *uinneag*, though this may have been inserted later; neither of the two panes opens. (All the other windows in the building are fixed roof lights, *fairleis*, in the thickness of the thatch.) The stone-flagged floor was once covered with linoleum, whilst the walls and entire roof were wallpapered; in order to make the roof take the paper, several planks and bits of boxes were nailed along the rafters, and across the hipped end. The wallpaper once hid from view the re-used boat tiller in the roof.

Two of the three box beds, *leapannan dhuinte*, are accessed from the bedroom. They are curtained and have knitted covers. When the house was lived in, there was a table with two leaves, a cupboard, chest, *ciste*, dresser for clothes, and clock, *uaireadair*, on the wall beside the window. A shelf above the door contained a variety of tins and odds and ends, and attached to the wooden partition wall was a Tilly-lamp, used before electricity was introduced in the 1950s.

The existence of a separate bedroom is a sign that no. 42 is of quite recent construction. In older blackhouses, the living room was used for sleeping as well as living in. The younger men normally slept in a circle around the hearth, with their feet towards the fire. If there were beds, these took the form of recesses in the side walls. These *crub* beds (*crub* literally means 'crouch') began to go out of use after about 1850, when closed wooden box-beds, such as those here in no. 42, became fashionable.

Above
1 The re-used boat tiller in the roof.

2 The bedroom in 1966, when there was still linoleum on the floor and paper on the walls and ceiling.

Right: One of the two box beds accessed from the bedroom. The third box bed opens on to the living room.

Below: Plan and section of the three box beds. The one on the left opens on to the living room.

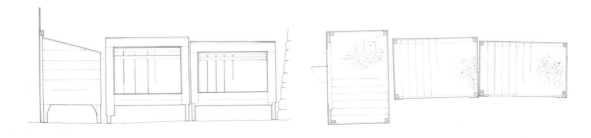

'The blackhouse is definitely the cosiest you can find'

'Chan eil àite air thalamh cho dachaigheil ris an taigh-dubh'

From a young girl's reminiscences recorded in *West Side Story*, 1964

Right: Pendulum clock.

THE BYRE *An bathaich*

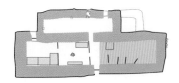

The byre, *bathaich*, is entered through a wooden partition to the right of the front door. It has cattle stalls, *stailichean*, along one side separated by three wooden partitions, formed of vertical wooden planks nailed to an angled member. There are no troughs; food for the cattle was simply laid into the forestall. The cattle were tethered to an upright wooden pole fixed against the wall. The floor of the stalls is raised slightly higher than the main earth floor, where a central drain, *eisir*, channelled the urine through a hole in the gable, *toll lodain*, to the outside. There is a wooden loose-box for calves to the left of the byre door as you enter.

Opposite page: The byre viewed from the entrance area.

Left: The cattle stalls. The beasts spent most of the summer at the shielings up in the hills. They only lived here in the winter.
In 1960 there was just one cow and her calf in residence.

Formerly, it was the custom in blackhouses to let the manure accumulate in the byre throughout the winter. In spring, instead of removing it laboriously through the front door, the gable end was broken open. This opening, in some cases sealed with turf, was called the 'horse hole', *toll each*, since this is where the cart or horse creels were loaded with dung. There is no evidence for such an opening here in no. 42 Arnol, which again points to its relatively late building date. Instead, the manure was cleared out as it accumulated.

Above: The byre looking towards the end gable.

THE BARN *An sabhal*

The barn, *sabhal*, lies parallel to the house and byre, with its own roof but sharing a common wall. It never extended the full length of the house and byre, however, and has also subsequently been shortened. A door in the wall opposite the front door leads into it and in line there is a low, blocked-up opening in the outer barn wall. This was the winnowing hole, *toll fasgnaidh*, set in line with the other doors to ensure a through-draught for winnowing.

The top end of the barn is floored with wooden planks as a base for the corn sheaves. There is a roof light, *uinneag tughaidh*, in the hipped end here. When sheaves were required from the stackyard, *lodhlann*, at the end of the house, it was the custom to open up the thatch around the window and pitch them in there. In the middle section, the smooth clay floor was where the grain was thrashed and winnowed. The flail, *suist*, used for thrashing, has three parts – a handstaff, *log*, a souple or beater, *buailtean*, (which was thicker and shorter than the handstaff) and a looped thong, *sail shuiste* (often of sheepskin) to link the other parts. It was swung over the shoulder or upper arm to beat out the grain from the ears of the sheaves. Afterwards, winnowing with a shallow circular sieve or riddle, *criathar*, was necessary to get rid of the chaff and broken straw, before the grain was taken to the kiln to be dried for grinding.

The potatoes were also stored here, (whence the name 'potato corner', *cuil bhuntata*), as were sickles and scythes, spades, rakes, peat-cutting irons and other small hand-tools, barrels and chests holding food for the hens and animals, and fleeces from the annual wool clip awaiting sale.

A wooden partition separates the outer part of the barn, which has its own exterior door. This was the 'ewes corner', *cuil-nan-othaisgean*, where they could shelter at lambing time.

Right: The top end of the barn. The roof light at the end was also used to load sheaves from the stackyard outside.

Below

1 Sheep on the croft in 2004. In 1966 the MacLeod family at no. 42 had eight breeding ewes, three other sheep and six lambs.

2 The 'potato corner'.

...🚶 Leave the blackhouse by the back door.

OUTSIDE THE BLACKHOUSE

Immediately outside the back door, down and to the left, is the blocked-up winnowing hole, and, beyond, the stackyard, *an iodhlann*, where the corn sheaves were stacked in rigs, *cruachan*. Along and to the right of the back door are the footings of the original south end of the barn. Although the present south gable of the barn is relatively new, it is a comment on the nature of the building stone that no appreciable difference can be seen between this and the older walling. The peat stack, *cruach mhònach*, lies nearby.

Around the corner of the byre are five stone steps, *staidhre*, protruding from the wall. These gave access to the ledge, *tobhta*, running around the outside edge of the walls. The ledge made it easier to carry out roof repairs as well as the wholesale rethatching that took place regularly. The thick layer of grassy sods on the ledge also made good eating for sheep, and it was even known for potatoes to be grown there!

Above: Section through the house (1) and barn (2).

Below: The back door.

THE WALLS

The walls have an inner and an outer skin of stone, and a central core, *uatabac*, of peat-mould and earth. The rafters rest on the inner face of the wall, and the thatch comes down as far as the core. Water shed from the roof percolates through the core, helping to improve its insulating qualities against both cold and wind.

Above: The blackhouse at no. 42 viewed from across the stackyard.

Bottom

1 The peat stack near the back door.

2 The steps at the end of the byre gave access to the roof, making maintenance and replacement much easier.

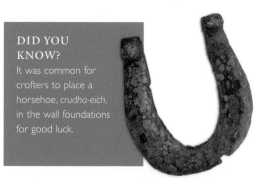

DID YOU KNOW?
It was common for crofters to place a horsehoe, *crudha-eich*, in the wall foundations for good luck.

'The thatch was made from oat straw,
it was replaced regularly. The old thatch
went to the fields for fertiliser'

'Bha an tughadh air a dhèanamh de chonnlach. Bhithte ga
ùrachadh bho àm gu àm. Bha an seann tughadh air a chur
air an fhearann mar thodhar.'

THE ROOF

The roof itself has been restored since the house was abandoned. The chief difference is that, when the house was occupied, the byre roof sagged (see the photo on page 3) in the way most byre-ends of blackhouses in the area sagged, perhaps because fewer tie-beams were used in this part - a cost-cutting measure because of the scarcity of timber, but also because the thatch was possibly not removed annually. To stop the sagging, the owner erected two upright poles in the middle of the floor; one actually sprang from the byre drain. These have since been removed, and the byre roof raised to match the height of the house roof.

The roof timbers are partly covered with heathery sods, *sgrathan*, overlapping like fish scales. The thatch, *tughadh*, formerly of bere-straw (now, as a rule, of oat-straw), was laid from eaves to ridge in shaken-out bunches, and fastened down by a fishing-net and ropes, *siomain*, formerly of heather, now of coir-yarn. The ends of the ropes go round anchor stones, *acraichean*, lying 300mm up from the wall-head. Another row of stones, not fixed to the ropes, is set between these and the wall-head.

At the apex of each hip is a protruding 'raven-stick', *maide fithich*, which served as an anchor for the ropes holding the thatch on the hip. The hipped roof, intended to make it more wind-resistant, means that the underlying rafters have to be arranged in a particular way. A centre beam, *a' chorr*, whose extension upwards through the thatch is used as an anchor for the ropes, links the middle of the gable and the roof-ridge. A pair of V-shaped members, *an roinn-oisinn*, stretch from each corner of the gable and side-walls to the roof-ridge.

There is no chimney or smoke-hole in the roof at no. 42 Arnol. This is a relic of the old tradition of allowing the thatch to become as impregnated with soot as possible, so that it could be removed regularly and used to fertilise the fields.

Opposite page top
Rethatching the roof was a regular task.

Opposite page bottom
1 The byre roof.

2 An anchor stone.

3 Working on the roof.

4 One of the 'raven-sticks'.

Above: Implements used for repairing and replacing the roof thatch.

Below: Heather rope.

THE BLACKHOUSE AT NO. 39 ARNOL

As you approach the ruined blackhouse, you pass through a stone and turf field wall stretching back up the hill towards the centre of the township. This wall marked the boundary between the croft land (beyond the wall) and the inbye, or inner pasture, where the animals grazed.

Standing outside the front door of no. 39, you will immediately see that this blackhouse differs from no. 42 in one important respect – it has three units in parallel, not two, a clear indication that it is older, though by how much is difficult to determine.

The extra unit is the front one – the entrance porch, *fosglan*, that served as a sort of utility room. This area was normally quite short, but here it is almost as long as the central unit housing the living room and byre. Strangely, the left-hand end of this first unit has a room that is no longer accessible, either from the porch, the house or from outside.

In most other respects, no. 39 is similar to no. 42. Passing through the entrance, you enter the heart of the building. On the left is the byre, and to the right the living room. The step separating the two areas is also to the left, indicating that the entrance entered directly into the living area. This too is unusual for it was more normal to enter the byre first. The current arrangement may be a later modification. Another change was made to the far end of the living room, which has clearly been extended. The new end gable also has a generous-sized window, another improvement. The alteration seems to be associated with creating a separate bedroom off the living room.

The third unit, at the rear of the house, was the barn. Unlike no. 42, which has a full-height door at the rear for human and animal access, the byre here has only the low winnowing hole. This too is a sign that no. 39 is older, for the only entrance into the traditional blackhouse was at the front. Immediately beyond the barn is the stackyard, and the white house that replaced no. 39 as the family residence.

... 🚶 Cross the road in front of no. 42 Arnol and head for the now roofless and ruined blackhouse at no. 39 Arnol.

Above: The interior of the blackhouse at no. 39 looking from the byre end towards the living room. The roof of the blackhouse at no. 42 rises up in the background.

Opposite page: The ruined and roofless blackhouse at no. 39 Arnol. The 'white house' that replaced it as the family residence from the 1920s stands behind it (to the left). The building beyond the 'white house', that replaced the blackhouse at no. 42 in 1966, is now the visitor centre.

Right: Reconstruction of no. 39 as it may have looked after the alterations to the living room and bedroom. *Drawn by Bruce Walker.*

THE WHITE HOUSE AT NO. 39 ARNOL

The two-storey building beside the ruined blackhouse at no. 39 is instantly recognisable as a house we today are more used to, and more comfortable with. It has solid walls, windows that actually open, a pitched roof and chimneys. It was built, as far as we can tell, in the 1920s. Unlike some other 'white houses' in Arnol, which were built as extensions to blackhouses, this one began as a free-standing, and stand-alone, dwelling.

Immediately inside the front door is a small hallway, with two doors leading off – one to the left into the living room, the other off to the right into the kitchen (but also including a box-bed). Straight ahead, a steep timber stair leads upstairs to a good-sized loft. Clearly, the intention had been to make two rooms up here – there are two fireplaces, both now blocked – but this was apparently never done.

Though the house feels comfortable enough, it seems it did not immediately find favour with the new residents, who apparently soon moved back into the blackhouse and rented out the 'white house'! A moment or two inside the latter, though, soon hints at the reason for this change of heart – the place is very damp.

The solid walls, with no damp-proof course, draw up the moisture from the boggy ground beneath, but because the outside walls are rendered over with impervious cement that moisture has nowhere to go but 'in the way' to the wallpaper. The problem is exacerbated by the drainage ditch running past the front door, which in rainy weather overflows into the hallway.

Nevertheless, the 'white house' continued to be inhabited until 1976, when the elderly lady living there was moved to a new home.

Above: The kitchen stove.

Below
1 The kitchen.

2 Clock.

3 Radio.

4 The living room.

THE BLACK HOUSE
Peigi Morrison

Standing so still, solidly, silently,
Dreaming of days gone by,
Each wall protecting a haven of secrets,
Never to be known again.
Who knows what conversations were had here,
What meals were cooked, what children played,
These walls reveal no secrets,
Standing solidly, silently.
Look closely and you'll see
The cailleach of long ago, dressed in black,
The blue eyes youthful in a wrinkled face,
Hunched over the warm peat fire.
The old collie lies crouched in the corner,
Reminiscing about his working days,
Rounding up sheep for his master, the bodach,
Now cold in his grave.
Nobody lives in this blackhouse now,
Children play there only for fun.
It stands in the field, alone and forgotten,
Standing solidly, silently.

(reproduced by courtesy of Peigi Morrison)

The croft at no. 42 Arnol today,
and a selection of archive
images of crofting life in and
around Arnol in the 1930s.
The MacLeod's family bible
is still in its dresser drawer
in the living room at no. 42.

LEABHRAICHEAN
AN
T-SEANN TIOMNAIDH
AGUS AN
TIOMNAIDH NUAIDH;
AIR AN TARRUING
O NA CEUD CHANAINIBH
CHUM GAIDHLIG ALBANNAI

John MacLeod
42 Aonal
Barvas
Stornoway

THE STORY OF ARNOL TOWNSHIP &
THE ISLAND BLACKHOUSE

I n Arnol the modern stone and lime or concrete-block dwelling houses roofed with slate, corrugated iron or tarred felt lie alongside older straw-thatched blackhouses. In such a township, a strong impression is given of looking two ways in time. On the one hand, there is the present that has not yet shaken down properly. On the other, there is the past, whose traces are still clear enough to suggest a much more functionally integrated system of communal existence. Yet this past too is very recent, for the linear arrangement of blackhouses and later 'white houses' along the roads of these crofting townships is little more than a century old. The previous settlement was down by the sea.

Above: Tractors replaced traditional manpower from the 1960s.

Above: Arnol township in 1937, photographed by E C Curwen.

Left: Arnol township today.

Right

1 An Arnol cow.

2 Arnol township on its ridge.

'OLD' ARNOL

The original site of Arnol was in the area above the rocky beach called Mol a' Chladaich, immediately to the north of Loch Arnol. Here the ruins of small, oval-ended stone houses are still visible. No doubt they date from and beyond the eighteenth century. Certainly, by 1753, 12 families were living here, according to estate records.

The homes lie on an accumulation of layers of sand, varying in depth, in which successive occupation layers are marked by pottery going back at least 2000 years. On this site, there was easy access to fish and fowl of the sea and the loch. In the hollow behind the little settlement lay the community's fields, still outlined by stone or built up on their lower edges to make level beds or platforms. A large rounded stone, prominent from its white colour, was used by the young lads as a trial for their growing strength. The stock of sheep, cattle and horses – and perhaps at one time goats – grazed on the slopes of Cnoc a'Charnain, Cnoc na Glas Bhuaile, Cnoc Mor Arnol and beyond.

It was a good site in summer. But when the winter storms swept in it was exposed, prone to erosion and liable also to be overwhelmed by beach boulders heaping up. This accumulation also made it difficult to drain the boggy area in the hollow behind the houses. Here, no doubt, was the peat they used for fuel, gradually exhausted through the centuries. Shortage of fuel in the immediate vicinity, coupled with an expanding population in the eighteenth century, were amongst the main factors that led to the re-siting of the township a little inland. Similar moves from sites hard by the shore were made by other Lewis townships, including nearby Shawbost.

Above: The shore at 'old' Arnol is strewn with Lewisian gneiss boulders, Britain's oldest

Left: The site of 'old' Arnol, down by the beach at Mol a' Chladaich.

Right: Map showing 'old' Arnol relative to the present township.

✳ Mills (medieval)
━ Croftland
━ Inner pasture

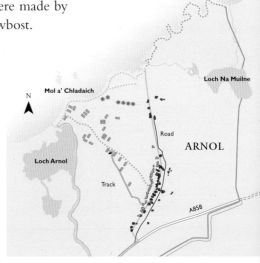

'The Arnol blackhouse was built just over
100 years ago, but belongs to a tradition
reaching back many centuries'

'Chaidh taigh-dubh Arnoil a thogail o chionn 100 bliadhna,
ach buinidh e do traidisean a tha a' dol air ais iomadh linn.'

'NEW' ARNOL

The move inland was instigated by the landlord, Mackenzie of Seaforth, in 1795 - an early attempt at agricultural 'improvement', whereby the older communal working of the land, the 'runrig' system, was to be replaced by the working of individual crofts. By this means, so the theory went, the tenant had a more secure 'hold' on his croft, giving him the incentive to 'improve' it year on year; it also enabled the landlord to calculate and collect his rents more easily.

There have been three 'new' Arnols since 1795. The first was strung out on either side of a track leading north-west from the ridge where the present township lies, down the slope towards Cnoc a'Charnain. It even had a schoolhouse, completed by 1835. In 1848, the township was described as 'a small township of miserably made huts... built of stone and peat sods and thatched with straw and heather'. By 1853, all but the schoolhouse were ruined. In less than 50 years the township was moved yet again.

The move up to the ridge was prompted by the arrival on the Lewis scene of Sir James Matheson, a successful businessman, who had purchased the debt-ridden Mackenzie family's Lewis estates in 1844 and immediately set about 'improving' them. These included Arnol. By 1853, the second 'new' Arnol had been established on the ridge, more or less on the alignment of the present one. But this too proved transitory, and scarcely any of that township's blackhouses survive today. However, the distinctive pattern of its croftlands does, for although the lines of stob-and-wire fencing are modern, the boundaries they define date back to 1849.

Right: Arnol township from the air in 1971. The old blackhouses. mostly roofless, stand alongside the later 'white houses'.

Opposite page: The view up the track from 'old' to 'new' Arnol.

'NEW' ARNOL

The relocation of the township to its third, and present, location took place around 1880, and was most likely prompted by Sir James Matheson's death in 1878. Regulations, called Articles of Set, issued by the new landlord offered crofters leases guaranteed until 1893 provided they undertook improvements to their homes and changes to their crofting way of life. The result was that most crofters chose to relocate rather to renovate, which explains why the present alignment of blackhouses lies some 30 m east of the 1849 township and why so little of the latter survives – the crofters simply took the stone from their old homes and built anew.

When the township moved to its present location, it was still blackhouses that were erected at first. At the same time, a number of houses were put up by squatters on the common grazing to the east, leading to a slightly ragged pattern of settlement.

Above: A cow grazes in the township.

Top: Blackhouses and 'white houses' stand alongside each other in Arnol township.

'Change is an inevitable part of life, to be accepted not deplored.'

'Tha atharrachadh dòigh-beatha do-sheachanta is feumar gabhail ris.'

According to the evidence given by Norman Campbell, crofter in Arnol, to the Napier Commission looking into crofting conditions in 1883, the number of families paying rent in the township had increased from 19 to 45, with ten more having no land. This increase was said to be the natural increase of the local population, only one or two families having come in from outside.

There were no restrictions on the siting of houses, least of all for the squatters on the common grazings. Another witness at that same Inquiry told how one man had gone to Stornoway to pay his rent, having missed rent-collection day, only to find that the croft rent had already been paid by a new tenant; when the man arrived back in Arnol, he found to his horror that 'the new entrant [had] built a house right in front of the old man's door so that he could scarcely enter it with a creel of peats on his back'!

Above: A rare two-storey 'white house'.

BLACKHOUSES ON THE WEST SIDE OF LEWIS

All homes built in Arnol up to 1900 were blackhouses. Originally these drystone, double-walled buildings were simply called *taighean*, 'houses'. Then a new type of house, with single-thickness walls cemented with lime-mortar, was introduced from the mainland 150 years ago. It presented such a contrast that people coined the term *taigh-geal*, 'white house'. The term *taigh-dubh*, 'black house', was then applied to the older houses.

Above: No. 42 Arnol in 1966, shortly after the MacLeod family had moved out.

Left: Inside another Lewis blackhouse, 1934.

The adoption of the name 'blackhouse' marked the beginning of the end of a building tradition that goes back into the Viking period. No. 42 Arnol, built around 1880, is an excellent example of the transition, for though many of its features match those of earlier houses, others diverge. Even though Lewis has been more resistant to change than most other areas, nevertheless changing fashions, altered social attitudes, estate and local authority regulations, and government legislation, have all had their effect.

The strength of the tradition is emphasised more than anything else by the fact that blackhouses were being built in considerable numbers in the late nineteenth century. In fact, few surviving examples ante-date the nineteenth century, though the ruins of older ones can still be found. From these, and from printed descriptions, it can be seen that even within this apparently rather inflexible building form, variation was to be found.

DID YOU KNOW?

Eighteenth- and early nineteenth-century blackhouses were not necessarily built solidly of stone, but often of peat sods lined internally with stones, which is why relatively few examples survive.

Some of the differences can be understood by contrasting no. 42 and no. 39 Arnol. No. 42 is a simplified form of the older type, which had more units, usually three in parallel, with just one entrance. Although the core of the blackhouse remained the same at all periods - the freely inter-communicating byre and house - in the earlier examples the entrance into the living area was normally through the byre, as at no. 39.

SEED-TIME AND HARVEST

The rocky nature of the land meant that crofters had to clear it of stones before cultivation. This they did by piling up clearance heaps. They then scraped the thin soil together into rigs or 'lazybeds', *feannagan*, using a light spade rather than the heavier caschrom 'crooked spade'. Even today, the caschrom is unknown as a working tool in the west side of Lewis.

There was much more land under cultivation than today, and traces of old cultivation beds show that some of the hill common was once under the spade. The crops were oats, bere (an old form of barley), hay and potatoes. For fertiliser, seaweed was used, and the manure that had accumulated in the byre over the winter.

By early May, as soon as the beasts were taken to the summer pasture, the end wall of the byre was broken out to facilitate the removal of the dung, by then about 300 mm deep. It was loaded onto cart, horse-back or human back.

The temporary nature of this gable, *toll each*, can still be seen on surviving blackhouses. Crofters also stripped the soot-blackened thatch off their dwelling-end roofs and spread that on the fields too. The regulations laid down by the estate in 1879 tried to put a stop to both practices: 'the thatch or covering not to be stripped off or removed for manure... in the byre a gutter to be formed for manure, which shall be regularly removed to a dung heap outside'. By the end of that century both were effectively past history.

Oats and bere were cut by sickle, *corran*, and bound into sheaves by hand on the knee with straw bands; each sheaf contained two good handfuls of straw. They were then set up in stooks, *adagan*, and left to dry in the fields before being taken home to be built into small, circular stacks, *cruachan*, in the stackyard adjacent to the barn where the crop was thrashed. Hay was cut, dried and stacked in much the same way. Potatoes were lifted by a method that is almost unique to Lewis. This involved a kind of adze-shaped mattock, *croman*, with a short wooden handle. The worker moved along the drill, picking out each stem and spreading the tubers with the blade before gathering them into a pail which, when full, was emptied into a creel, *cliabh*.

Above: Sieve used to winnow the freshly thrashed grain.

Right: Harvesting oats with a sickle, Isle of Lewis, c1950.

Right
1 A field of stooks.

2 Stacks.

3 Seaweed from the beach was used for fertiliser.

4 The stackyard at no. 42 Arnol.

PEAT

A harvest of another kind was peat, *moine*, which provided winter fuel for the fire. Peat is one natural resource that exists in great plenty in Lewis, but constant peat-cutting over the centuries has had the effect of continually moving the banks away from the townships. Today, the Arnol peat-banks lie over 1.5 km away. A compensating factor, however, was that the clearance of peat exposed the underlying mineral soils, which eventually could be reclaimed for grazing or cropping.

It is a remarkable sight to visit Arnol about October, when the peats are home and stacked by the houses, their dark bulk almost dwarfing the buildings themselves.

Above: Peat-cutters' afternoon Mr. and Mrs. Mackay, of Dalbeag south of Arnol, stop for a breath

Top: The peat stack at no. 42

A crofting household of four persons, burning nothing but peat, would use approximately 15,000 peats in a year. A good man working the peat-spade, *tairisgeir*, could cast 1000 a day, so that he had to spend a minimum of 15 days, given continuous good weather, at this job. Later, the peats had to be set up to dry, then transported home and stacked. Peat work probably occupied about a month of the crofter's year, and unless a good surplus of labour was available, this could seriously interfere with the working of the croft.

In practice, neighbours and relatives worked at the job together – and still do – usually in pairs, one cutting and the other casting. This way the job is carried out faster and with enjoyment.

Above:
(1) Loading peats at Arnol today and (2) loading peats at Arnol in the 1930s (3) an Arnol peat-bank (4) peats (5) a peat stack with spade, and (6) returning from peat-cutting at Arnol in 1937; note the bare feet.

KILNS AND MILLS

After the harvest had been safely gathered, the work of processing it began. The first stage was to thrash it in the barn, using the flail, to separate the ears from the straw. Next the grain was winnowed to clear away the chaff and empty husks, then the ears were dried in preparation for grinding. Small quantities of grain would be dried over the fire before being ground in a quern, or hand-mill, *brath*.

Larger quantities were dried in a stone-built corn-drying kiln, *ath*, of which there were at least four in Arnol. These were separate buildings with one straight and one rounded gable. The kiln itself was in the rounded end. Three large bags of grain could be dried at a time, in 6-8 hours, with three dryings a day at the busy period when everyone was eager to get the first corn of the season dried and ground into fresh meal.

Above: Oats.

Top: The horizontal water powered mill at Shawbost, just south of Arnol, in 1937. The mill has since been restored and is well worth a visit.

The grain had to be turned regularly by hand to achieve even drying, and when the time came, the man in charge, the *bodach*, tested it with his teeth to see if it was ready. One drying could yield two bags of oatmeal.

Once dried, the grain was taken for grinding to the mill, *muileann*. These lay at the edge of the township beside the running water that powered them. The burn flowing from the two lochs to the north-east, Loch na Muilne, 'mill loch', and Loch Bheag na Muilne, 'little mill loch', at one time turned four or five little mills; Allt na Muilne, 'mill burn', south-west of Arnol, suggests the site of others. The last mill used by the crofters lay beside the River Ereray close to where it flows out of Loch Urrahag.

The earlier and much smaller type of mill had a horizontally turning water-wheel linked directly to the upper grind-stone without gearing; whence its name 'horizontal mill'. Water from the lade was channelled by a narrow chute onto the blades of the wheel, which turned below the floor of the mill in a lower chamber. Inside the mill, a wooden hopper suspended above the mill-stones was filled with grain which then trickled out onto the upper mill-stone. Vibrations communicated to the hopper by a stick rubbing on the turning mill-stone helped to ensure a regular flow.

Crofters used such mills once or twice a year, several families sometimes sharing one mill, and it was said that enough grain could be ground in 48 hours to last a family for the whole year. The problem was not the grinding, granted a plentiful supply of water, but the difficulty of getting enough grain dried and dehusked in advance for grinding.

Below left: Interior of a mill at Bragar c1920. The wooden hopper and the mill-stones below were typical machinery in a Lewis mill.

'Shieling time is the most delightful time of the year... the time of the healthy heather bed and the healthy outdoor life... of the moorland breeze and the warm sun... of the curds and the cream of the heather milk...'

'B' e àm dol chun na h-àirigh an t-àm a b'fheàrr sa bhliadhna air an tuath... àm na leapa-fraoich fhallain agus nae dòigh-beatha fhallain... oiteag na mòintich agus blàths na grèine... an gruth agus uachdar a'bhainne'

Alexander Carmichael, from *Carmina Gadelica, Ortha nan Gaidheal*, 1900

SHIELINGS AND SOUMINGS

The amount of byre accommodation in the Arnol blackhouses, and the small number of cattle kept by today's crofters, testifies to the changes in emphasis that have taken place since the present township was built around 1880. Sheep and cattle have changed places in importance, and this is a change that is far more fundamental and far-reaching than might appear at first sight, for it marks more than anything else the end of the older traditional way of life.

When cattle played the chief part in the economy, the system of transhumance – the annual movement of cows, calves and people, along with the formerly much smaller stock of sheep, from the croft to the shieling, *airidh*, up in the moorland to the south – was an integral part of the cycle of subsistence and survival.

But in the course of the nineteenth century sheep came to absorb the hill grazings more and more and the use of shielings gradually died out. This ancient practice continued longer in Lewis than in any other part of Britain, and shielings remained quite common till 1939. Even as late as 1960, one Arnol man still spent the summer at his shieling with his two cows.

Above: Inside Mrs. MacSween's shieling in Gleann Bhruthadail in 1937; Mrs. MacSween sits on the right.

Top: A shieling in Gleann Bhruthadail, belonging to an Arnol crofting family. Arnol township is just visible on the horizon.

The Arnol shielings were clustered between Gleann Bhragair and Gleann Bhruthadail. They were occupied from early in May until after the harvest. The older shieling-huts were built mostly of peat and are barely noticeable among the heather. But good examples remain of the later, stone-built shielings. These are oval-shaped, measure around 3 m by 2 m internally, with two low entrance doorways, a fireplace at one end and little storage cupboards in the walls.

Above: Families from other shielings pose outside Mrs. MacSween's shieling in 1937.

Whilst the animals, the women and the young folk were at the shieling, the crops grew unmolested in the unfenced fields and cultivation beds around the township. With the women and children away at the shieling, now was a good time to strip the soot-blackened thatch from the blackhouse roofs and re-use it as fertiliser.

When the beasts were not at the summer shielings, they grazed on the common land around the township. A system known as 'souming' controlled the amount of stock allowed by each croft; no. 42 Arnol's 'souming' in 1960 was one cow and one 'follower', or calf, up to two years old, and seven sheep. In order to keep a balance between crofters whose stock-holding emphases varied, a system of equivalents was applied: 1 cow = 5 sheep; 1 horse = 2 cows or 10 sheep. A grazing committee, composed of the crofters themselves, looked after the 'souming'.

ON THE CROFT

Daily life on the croft began at dawn with the raking of the embers of the previous day's fire. The peat fire was the centre of family life and was never allowed to go out. Breakfast followed, usually a bowl of porage oats and milk, perhaps potatoes.

In the summer months, the fit older people and the elder children (pupils could leave school at the age of 12) went with the animals to the shieling, leaving the others to remain behind tending to the ripening crops. But when all were at home, there were many jobs to be done in addition to working the fields and tending the beasts. High on the list was milking the cows, which was done morning and night. A little went to the calf, the rest for family use.

The cream was skimmed off and put into a churn for making butter, for baking or for making cheese. There was also corn to be threshed and ground, creels and heather ropes to be made, and tools and nets to be mended.

One job, spinning and weaving wool, grew from being a domestic activity carried out mostly by women into an industry largely the preserve of men. In the nineteenth century, every blackhouse had its spinning-wheel and loom. But after World War I, as the Harris tweed industry developed, the introduction of the heavier 'flying shuttle' looms meant it was more appropriate work for men. By 1939, there were over 1000 such looms on Lewis alone, weaving wool dyed, carded and spun in a Stornoway factory. Abandoned blackhouses were ideal as weaving-sheds, sufficiently close to the white houses but with thick enough walls to deaden the racket made by the shuttles. By 1960, there were 13 full-time and eight part-time weavers in Arnol. Now there are just three.

Above: A lady spins wool outside her blackhouse near Stornoway, c1900.

Below: Harris tweed cloth.

Below left: A crofter from Shawbost township, near Arnol, at his hand loom weaving Harris tweed, c1950.

Opposite page: The spinning wheel in the living room at no. 42 Arnol.

You stoop your head as you enter the only door, and if you visit in March... you step upon a thick mass of wet cattle-bedding and dung, which has accumulated since the previous summer. Coming in from the light of day you stumble in the deep obscurity which is barely relieved by the single window of a foot square. You make your way over the spongy surface, and at length find yourself on firm ground as you approach the large peat fire burning on the middle of the floor, the smoke from which fills the whole house, and finds partial egress through the thatch for there is no chimney... Overhead the cackling of hens, which are striving for the warmest roost near the fire, attracts your notice... and dimly visible through the smoke are two pallet beds at the inner end of the apartment. The lowing of the calf at the far end of the house... leads you to grope your way thither, and you are told that at present the rest of the beasts are grazing outside.

A graphic description of blackhouse conditions, contained in a Report by the Royal Commission on the Housing of the Working Classes, 1885. The report led directly to the 1886 Crofters' Holding Act.

1886 CROFTERS' HOLDING ACT

- SECURITY OF TENURE SO LONG AS THE CROFTER PAID HIS RENT;

- THE RIGHT TO A FAIR RENT;

- THE RIGHT TO COMPENSATION, ON LEAVIN FOR IMPROVEMENTS CARRIED OUT;

- THE RIGHT TO BEQUEATH THE TENANCY.

FROM BLACKHOUSE TO WHITE HOUSE

The impact of the 1886 Crofters' Holding Act on Arnol was felt almost immediately, and remains evident today. The crofters, knowing they now had some sort of security of tenure, felt able to improve their crofts. Larger blackhouses appeared, particularly on the former inner pasture, or inbye, to the east of the present road. The road itself, built in the early 1890s, drew new houses to it like a magnet and gave the township its characteristically linear layout. The expansion eastward across the road was the last of the township's numerous moves. Future improvements focused on the houses themselves.

Estate regulations had tried to impose the separation of byre from dwelling, but crofters were reluctant to change. An 1886 report refers to the obstinate retention of cattle under the roof. In 1893 the Lewis District Committee minuted a regulation requiring complete separation of byre and dwelling end by a wall, with no internal communication; they even instructed a sanitary inspector to institute legal proceedings if need be.

Under such pressure, the crofters had no option but to conform - eventually. They began by building stone partitions between byre and living area, often taking the opportunity to put the fireplace in the separating gable. Later, they built extensions onto their blackhouses, usually one-storeyed and housing bedroom(s). During the 1920s, the first two-storeyed white houses began to appear, some still stubbornly linked internally to the blackhouse, others such as no. 39 physically separate.

But even the new free-standing white houses, with all the additional space they offered, largely continued to support the living space in the blackhouse rather than supplant it. Only after World War II did the formal break come and the white house become the residence; now the only animal allowed inside the house was the cat! Even so, nine Arnol blackhouses were still being inhabited, by humans and animals, as recently as 1960; they included no. 42.

Above

1 A ruined blackhouse in Arnol.

2 The blackhouse at no. 42 Arnol.

3 Arnol township today, with its mix of blackhouses and white houses.

Opposite page: The view from the entrance area into the living room in no. 42 Arnol.

ARNOL TODAY

In 1962, the Scottish Land Court granted Barvas Estates permission to resume from crofting no. 42 Arnol. The area was then feued to the Ministry of Works (now Historic Scotland), who wished to preserve it. In 1966, the family moved into their new white house adjacent.

In 1966 the family worked 1.9 ha (2.7 acres) of land. In addition, they had access to other ground on the common grazing land. They grew oats, potatoes and turnips, turned the soil with a borrowed tractor, and used chemical fertiliser together with byre manure. In the garden they grew cabbages, carrots and the odd lettuce. But still 'living in' with them was one cow and calf, eight breeding ewes and 26 chickens. When the family left, so too did their animals – but as they exited through the door, they went their separate ways.

Above: Sheep grazing in Arnol township.

Top: The blackhouse at no. 42 Arnol looking over Port Arnol to Aird Bheag Bràgair. The blackhouse seems to mirror the shape of the distant headland.

What of the township? In 1960, the electoral roll listed 155 voters sharing 12 surnames; MacLeod was the most common. The male population between the ages of 15 and 65 stood at 82. Only eight were full-time crofters, 13 were weavers and 12 were in the Merchant Navy; the rest were either permanently away or unemployed. In this respect, Arnol was characteristic of West-side communities, but it also had its own distinctive mark. More blackhouses have survived here than in most places, marking the tightly-knit nature of the community; between 1939 and 1960 only 13 people are recorded as having left by migration.

Of all those blackhouses, no. 42 stands alone as representing a lost age. Though little more than a century old, it admirably typifies the nature of both the change and conservatism that characterised the west side and other parts of Lewis until relatively recently.

Above: A 'thank you' card to Historic Scotland's stewards at Arnol from a grateful Primary 7 pupil from nearby Bragar School. Apart from finding the place a bit smoky, D.J. apparently had a great time and learned a lot.

'...some of them play the pipes... and the song and the dance and the merriment continued all night long under the moon on the green grass before the shieling door'

'...chluicheadh cuid aca a' phìob... agus bhiodh òrain, dannsa agus greadhnachas a' dol fad na h-oidhche fo sholas na gealaich air an fheur ghorm aig doras na h-àirigh.'

Alexander Carmichael, from *Carmina Gadelica, Ortha nan Gaidheal*, 1900

Arnol Blackhouse is one of six Historic Scotland sites situated in the Western Isles. (A selection of these sites is on the right.) For more information visit: **www.historic-scotland.gov.uk**

Why not visit our online shop: Tickets to all Historic Scotland monuments and a wide range of products, including guidebooks and souvenirs, can be ordered online at www.historic-scotland.gov.uk/shop

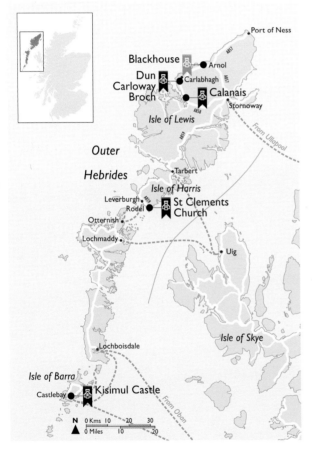

Facilities (Key)	
Reasonable wheelchair access	Shop
Car parking	Picnic area
Bus/coach parking	Interpretive display
Toilets	Admission charge

Calanais Standing Stones

12m W of Stornoway on A859
Open all year **Summer:** 10 - 6pm **Winter:** 10 - 4pm (Wed-Sat)
01851 621422
Approx 15 miles from Arnol
Facilities

Dun Carloway Broch

1.5m S of Carloway 16m NW of Stornoway on A858
Open all year
Contact Arnol Blackhouse for info 01851 710395
Approx 12 miles from Arnol
Facilities

Kisimul Castle

Isle of Barra reached by boat from Castlebay (5mins) - check weather
Open summer only
01871 810313
Approx 121 miles from Arnol
Facilities

St Clement's Church

At Rodel, Isle of Harris on A859
Open all year
Contact Arnol Blackhouse for info 01851 710395
Approx 70 miles from Arnol
Facilities